Hello Friends!

Places I Know

Imagine That!

Oh, What Fun!

Let's Go Outside

What a Funny Animal!

IMAGINATION
An Odyssey Through Language

Oh, What Fun!

Gail Heald-Taylor
General Consultant, Language Arts

 HARCOURT BRACE JOVANOVICH, PUBLISHERS

Orlando   San Diego   Chicago   Dallas

Printed in the United States of America

ISBN 0-15-332805-3

Acknowledgments

For permission to reprint copyrighted material, grateful acknowledgment is made to the following sources:

Child's Play (International) Ltd.: Quick as a Cricket by Audrey Wood, illustrated by Don Wood. © 1982 by M. Twinn.
Doubleday & Company, Inc. and The Society of Authors, as the literary representative of the Estate of Rose Fyleman: "Singing-Time" from *The Fairy Green* by Rose Fyleman. Copyright 1923 by George H. Doran.
E. P. Dutton, a division of NAL Penguin Inc.: "Quack! Quack! Quack!" from *Hand Rhymes,* collected and illustrated by Marc Brown. Copyright © 1985 by Marc Brown.
Macmillan Publishing Company: From *Over, Under & Through and Other Spatial Concepts* by Tana Hoban. Copyright © 1973 by Tana Hoban.
Arnold Spilka: Paint All Kinds of Pictures by Arnold Spilka. © 1963 by Arnold Spilka.

Art Credits

Lori Anderson: 22, 23, 24, 25; Marc Brown: 2, 3; James Buckley: 6, 7; Marie-Louise Gay: 4, 5; Arnold Spilka: 34-62; Don Wood: 8-21.

PHOTO CREDITS: Tana Hoban: 26-33

Cover: Tom Vroman

Contents

Hello Friends!

Places I Know

Imagine That!

Oh, What Fun!

Let's Go Outside

What a Funny Animal!

Quack! Quack! Quack!

A hand rhyme by Marc Brown

Five little ducks that I once knew,

Big ones, little ones, skinny ones, too.

But the one little duck with the

Feather on his back,

All he could do was, "Quack! Quack! Quack!"

All he could do was, "Quack! Quack! Quack!"

Down to the river they would go,

Waddling, waddling, to and fro.

But the one little duck with the

Feather on his back,

All he could do was, "Quack! Quack! Quack!"

All he could do was, "Quack! Quack! Quack!"

 Up from the river they would come.

Ho, ho, ho, ho, hum, hum, hum.

But the one little duck with the
Feather on his back,

All he could do was, "Quack! Quack! Quack!"

All he could do was, "Quack! Quack! Quack!"

Mix a Pancake

A poem by Christina Rossetti

Mix a pancake,
Stir a pancake,
    Pop it in the pan;
Fry the pancake,
Toss the pancake,—
    Catch it if you can.

Pictures by Marie-Louise Gay

Singing-Time

A poem by Rose Fyleman

I wake in the morning early
And always, the very first thing,
I poke out my head and I sit up in bed
And I sing and I sing and I sing.

Quick as a Cricket

From a story by Audrey Wood

I'm as quick as a cricket.

I'm as slow as a snail.

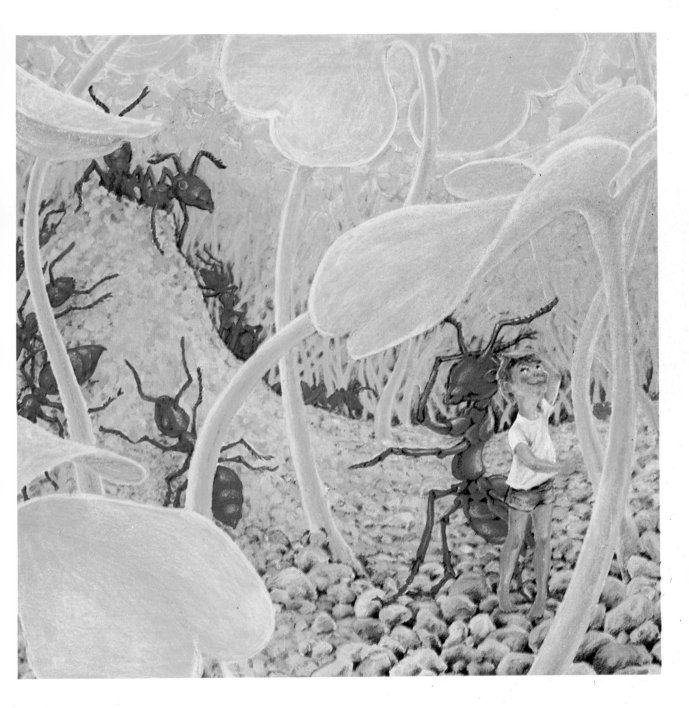

I'm as small as an ant.

I'm as large as a whale.

13

I'm as sad as a basset.

I'm as happy as a lark.

I'm as cold as a toad.

I'm as hot as a fox.

I'm as loud as a lion.

I'm as quiet as a clam.

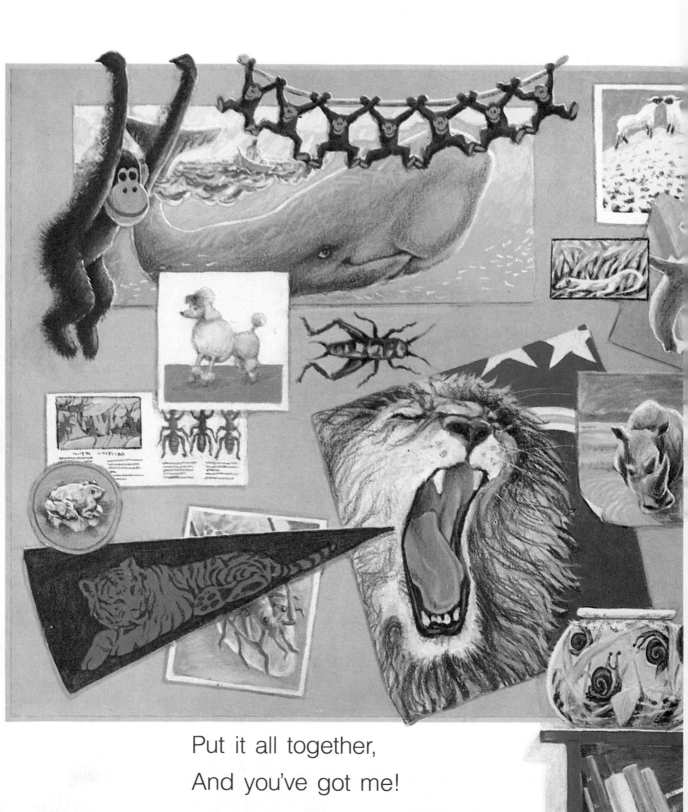

Put it all together,
And you've got me!

21

Connections

How Do They Feel?

over, under & through

by tana hoban

over

under

through

in

on

around

across

between

31

beside

below

Paint All Kinds of Pictures

Story and pictures by Arnold Spilka

Your pictures can be ANYTHING.

They can be very LARGE

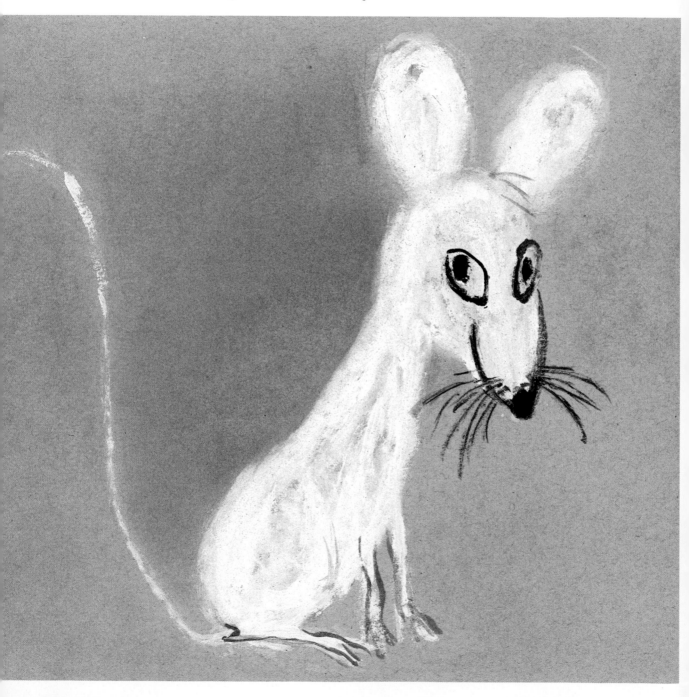

. . . or very small.

You can paint in colors

or black and white

or white and black.

Your pictures can be pretty

. . . or FUNNY

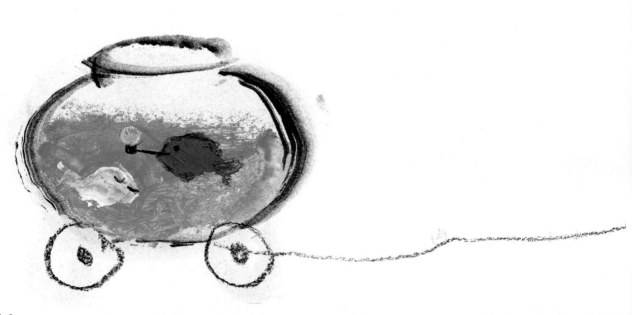

. . . or EXCITING.

They can be flowery pictures

51

or showery pictures.

You can paint a LOUD picture,

a quiet picture

or a lonely picture.

57

If you like fish you might make a
picture like this.

If you <u>don't</u> like fish you might
make a picture like this.

Even the designs you make

can show how you feel.

So you see each picture you paint is YOU in a way.
And you <u>can</u> paint all kinds of pictures.